BURY THE DEAD

BURY
THE DEAD

by
IRWIN SHAW

*"... what is this world that
you cling to it?"*

RANDOM HOUSE · NEW YORK

To My Mother

BURY THE DEAD

CAST OF CHARACTERS

PRIVATE DRISCOLL

PRIVATE MORGAN

PRIVATE LEVY

PRIVATE WEBSTER

PRIVATE SCHELLING

PRIVATE DEAN

JOAN BURKE

BESS SCHELLING

MARTHA WEBSTER

JULIA BLAKE

KATHERINE DRISCOLL

ELIZABETH DEAN

Generals One, Two and Three.

A Captain, a Sergeant, and four infantrymen, employed as a burial detail.

A Priest, a Rabbi, a Doctor.

A Reporter and an Editor

Two Whores

TIME

The second year of the war that is to begin tomorrow night.

SCENE

The stage is in two planes—in the fore-ground, the bare stage, in the rear, not too far back, going the entire length of the stage, a platform about seven feet above the level of the stage proper. No properties are used to adorn the stage save for some sandbags, whole and split, lying along the edge of the raised plat-form and some loose dirt also on the platform. The entire platform is painted dull black. It is lighted by a strong spotlight thrown along it at hip-height from the right wing. It is the only light on the stage. The platform is to represent a torn-over battlefield, now quiet, some miles behind the present lines, where a burial detail, standing in a shallow trench dug in the plat-form, so that the audience sees them only from the hip up, are digging a common grave to ac-commodate six bodies, piled on the right of the platform, wrapped in canvas. A sergeant stands on the right, on the edge of the grave, smoking. . . . The soldier nearest him, in the shallow trench, stops his digging. . . .

BURY THE DEAD

FIRST SOLDIER

Say, Sergeant, they stink.... (*Waving his shovel at the corpses*) Let's bury them in a hurry....

SERGEANT

What the hell do you think you'd smell like, after you'd been lyin' out for two days—a god-damn lily of the valley? They'll be buried soon enough. Keep digging.

SECOND SOLDIER
(*Scratching himself*)

Dig and scratch! Dig and scratch! What a war! When you're not diggin' trenches you're diggin' graves....

THIRD SOLDIER

Who's got a cigarette? I'll take opium if no-body's got a cigarette.

SECOND SOLDIER

When you're not diggin' graves you're scratchin' at fleas. By God, there're more fleas in this army than ...

FIRST SOLDIER

That's what the war's made for—the fleas. Somebody's got to feed 'em....

FOURTH SOLDIER

I used to take a shower every day. Can you imagine?

SERGEANT

All right, Mr. Lifebuoy, we'll put your picture in the *Saturday Evening Post*—in color!

SECOND SOLDIER

When you're not scratchin' at fleas, you're bein' killed. That's a helluva life for a grown man.

THIRD SOLDIER

Who's got a cigarette? I'll trade my rifle—if I can find it—for a cigarette. For Christ's sake, don't they make cigarettes no more? (*Leaning, melancholy, on his shovel*) This country's goin' to the dogs for real now. . . .

SERGEANT

Lift dirt, soldier. Come on! This ain't no vacation.

THIRD SOLDIER

(*Disregarding him*)

I heard of guys packin' weeds and cowflop into cigarettes in this man's army. They say it has a tang. (*Reflectively*) Got to try it some day. . . .

SERGEANT

Hurry up! (*Blowing on his hands*) I'm freezin' here. I don't want to hang around all night. I can't feel my feet no more. . . .

FOURTH SOLDIER

I ain't felt my feet for two weeks. I ain't had my shoes off in two weeks. (*Leaning on his shovel*) I wonder if the toes're still connected. I wear a 8A shoe. Aristocratic foot, the salesman always said. Funny—going around not even knowin' whether you still got toes or not. . . . It's not hygienic really. . . .

SERGEANT

All right, friend, we'll make sure the next war you're in is run hygienic.

FOURTH SOLDIER

In the Spanish-American War more men died of fever than . . .

FIRST SOLDIER

(*Beating viciously at something in the grave*) Get him! Get him! Kill the bastard!

FOURTH SOLDIER

(*Savagely*)

He's coming this way! We got him cornered!

FIRST SOLDIER

Bash his brains out!

SECOND SOLDIER

You got him with that one! (*All the soldiers in the grave beat at it, yelling demoniacally, triumphantly.*)

SERGEANT

(*Remonstrating*)

Come on now, you're wasting time. . . .

FIRST SOLDIER

(*Swinging savagely*)

There. That fixed him. The god-damn . . .

FOURTH SOLDIER

(*Sadly*)

You'd think the rats'd at least wait until the stiffs were underground.

FIRST SOLDIER

Did you ever see such a fat rat in your whole life? I bet he ate like a horse—this one.

SERGEANT

All right, all right. You're not fightin' the war against rats. Get back to your business.

FIRST SOLDIER

I get a lot more pleasure killin' rats than killin' them. (*Gesture toward the front lines.*)

SERGEANT

Rats got to live, too. They don't know no better.

FIRST SOLDIER

(*Suddenly scooping up rat on his shovel and presenting it to* SERGEANT)

Here you are, Sergeant. A little token of our regard from Company A.

SERGEANT

Stop the smart stuff! I don't like it.

FIRST SOLDIER

(*Still with rat upheld on shovel*)

Ah, Sergeant, I'm disappointed. This rat's a
fine pedigreed animal—fed only on the choicest
young men the United States's turned out in the
last twenty years.

SERGEANT

Come on, wise guy. (FIRST SOLDIER *goes right
on.*)

FIRST SOLDIER

Notice the heavy, powerful shoulders to this
rat, notice the well-covered flanks, notice the
round belly—bank clerks, mechanics, society-
leaders, farmers—good feeding—(*Suddenly he
throws the rat away*) Ah—I'm gettin' awful
tired of this. I didn't enlist in this bloody war
to be no bloody grave-digger!

SERGEANT

Tell that to the President. Keep diggin'.

SECOND SOLDIER

Say, this is deep enough. What're we supposed
to do—dig right down to hell and deliver them
over first-hand?

SERGEANT

A man's entitled to six feet a' dirt over his face.

We gotta show respect to the dead. Keep diggin'. . . .

FOURTH SOLDIER

I hope they don't put me too far under when my turn comes. I want to be able to come up and get a smell of air every once in so often.

SERGEANT

Stow the gab, you guys! Keep diggin'. . . .

FIRST SOLDIER

They stink! Bury them!

SERGEANT

All right, Fanny. From now on we'll perfume 'em before we ask you to put them away. Will that please you?

FIRST SOLDIER

I don't like the way they smell, that's all. I don't have to like the way they smell, do I? That ain't in the regulations, is it? A man's got a right to use his nose, ain't he, even though he's in this god-damn army. . . .

SERGEANT

Talk respectful when you talk about the army, you!

FIRST SOLDIER

Oh, the lovely army . . . (*He heaves up clod of dirt.*)

SECOND SOLDIER

Oh, the dear army ... (*He heaves up clod of dirt.*)

THIRD SOLDIER

Oh, the sweet army ... (*He heaves up clod of dirt.*)

FIRST SOLDIER

Oh, the scummy, stinking, god-damn army ... (*He heaves up three shovelfuls in rapid succession.*)

SERGEANT

That's a fine way to talk in the presence of death. . . .

FIRST SOLDIER

We'd talk in blank verse for you, Sergeant, only we ran out of it our third day in the front line. What do you expect, Sergeant, we're just common soldiers ...

SECOND SOLDIER

Come on. Let's put 'em away. I'm getting blisters big enough to use for balloons here. What's the difference? They'll just be turned up anyway, the next time the artillery wakes up. . . .

SERGEANT

All right! All right! If you're in such a hurry —put 'em in. . . . (*The soldiers nearest the right-hand edge of the grave jump out and start carrying the bodies over, one at each corner of the canvas. The other soldiers, still in the trench, take the bodies from them and carry them over to the other side of the trench, where they lay them down, out of sight of the audience.*)

SERGEANT

Put 'em in neat, there. . . .

FIRST SOLDIER

File 'em away alphabetically, boys. We may want to refer to them, later. The General might want to look up some past cases.

FOURTH SOLDIER

This one's just a kid. I knew him a little. Nice kid. He used to write dirty poems. Funny as hell. He don't even look dead. . . .

FIRST SOLDIER

Bury him! He stinks!

SERGEANT

If you think *you* smell so sweet, yourself, Baby, you oughta wake up. You ain't exactly a perfume-ad, soldier. (*Laughter.*)

THIRD SOLDIER

Chalk one up for the Sergeant.

FIRST SOLDIER

You ain't a combination of roses and wistaria, either, Sergeant, but I can stand you, especially

when you don't talk. At least you're alive.
There's something about the smell of dead ones
that gives me the willies. . . . Come on, let's pile
the dirt in on them. . . . (*The* SOLDIERS *scramble
out of the grave.*)

SERGEANT

Hold it.

THIRD SOLDIER

What's the matter now? Do we have to do a
dance around them?

SERGEANT

We have to wait for chaplains. . . . They gotta
say some prayers over them.

FIRST SOLDIER

Oh, for Christ's sake, ain't I ever going to get
any sleep tonight?

SERGEANT

Don't begrudge a man his prayers, soldier.
You'd want 'em, wouldn't you?

FIRST SOLDIER

God, no. I want to sleep peaceful when I go. . . .
Well, where are they? Why don't they come?
Do we have to stand here all night waiting for
those guys to come and talk to God about these
fellers?

THIRD SOLDIER

Who's got a cigarette? (*Plaintively.*)

SERGEANT

Attention! Here they are! (*A Roman-Catholic priest and a rabbi come in.*)

PRIEST

Is everything ready?

SERGEANT

Yes, Father...

FIRST SOLDIER

Make it snappy! I'm awful tired.

PRIEST

God must be served slowly, my son....

FIRST SOLDIER

He's gettin' plenty of service these days—and not so slow, either. He can stand a little rushin'....

SERGEANT

Shut up, soldier.

RABBI

Do you want to hold your services first, Father?

SERGEANT

There ain't no Jewish boys in there. (*Gesture to grave*) Reverend, I don't think we'll need you.

RABBI

I understand one of them is named Levy.

SERGEANT

Yes. But he's no Jew.

RABBI

With that name we won't take any chances. Father, will you be first?

PRIEST

Perhaps we had better wait. There is an Episcopal bishop in this sector. He expressed the desire to conduct a burial service here. He's doing that in all the sectors he is visiting. I think we had better wait for him. Episcopal bishops are rather sensitive about order....

RABBI

He's not coming. He's having his supper.

FIRST SOLDIER

What does God do while the bishop has his supper?

SERGEANT

If you don't keep quiet, I'll bring you up on charges.

FIRST SOLDIER

I want to get it over with! Bury them! They stink!

PRIEST

Young man, that is not the way to talk about one of God's creatures....

FIRST SOLDIER

If *that's* (*Gesture to grave*) one of God's creatures, all I can say is, He's slippin' . . .

PRIEST

Ah, my son, you seem so bitter. . . .

FIRST SOLDIER

For God's sake, stop talking and get this over
with. I want to throw dirt over them! I can't
stand the smell of them! Sergeant, get 'em to
do it fast. They ain't got no right to keep us up
all night. We got work to do tomorrow. . . .
Let 'em say their prayers together! God'll be
able to understand. . . .

PRIEST

Yes. There is really no need to prolong it. We
must think of the living as well as the dead. As
he says, Reverend, God will be able to understand. . . . (*He stands at the head of the grave,
chants the Latin prayer for the dead. The*
RABBI *goes around to the other end and recites
the Hebrew prayer. In the middle of it, a groan
is heard, low, but clear. The chants keep on.
Another groan is heard.*)

FIRST SOLDIER

(*While the Hebrew and Latin go on*)
I heard a groan. (*The* RABBI *and* PRIEST *con-
tinue*) I heard a groan!

SERGEANT

Shut up, soldier! (*The Latin and Hebrew go
on.*)

FIRST SOLDIER

(*Gets down on one knee by side of grave and listens. Another groan*)
Stop it! I heard a groan ...

SERGEANT

What about it? Can you have war without groans? Keep quiet! (*The prayers go on undisturbed. Another groan. The* FIRST SOLDIER *jumps into the grave.*)

FIRST SOLDIER

It's from here! Hold it! (*Screaming*) Hold it! Stop those god-damned parrots! (*Throws a clod of dirt at end of trench*) Hold it! Somebody down here groaned.... (*A head appears slowly above the trench rim at the left end, a man stands up, slowly facing the rear. All the men sigh—the service goes on.*)

SERGEANT

Oh, my God ...

FIRST SOLDIER

He's alive. ...

SERGEANT

Why the hell don't they get these things straight? Pull him out!

FIRST SOLDIER

Stop them! (*As the services go on*) Get them out of here! Live men don't need them. ...

SERGEANT

Please, Father, this has nothing to do with you. . . . There's been some mistake. . . .

PRIEST

I see. All right, Sergeant. (*He and* RABBI *join, hand in hand, and leave. Nobody notices them. All the men are hypnotically watching the man in the trench, arisen from the dead. The* CORPSE *passes his hand over his eyes. The men sigh—horrible, dry sighs. . . . Another groan is heard from the left side of trench.*)

FIRST SOLDIER
(*In trench*)

There! (*Pointing*) It came from there! I heard it! (*A head, then shoulders appear over the rim of trench at left side. The* SECOND CORPSE *stands up, passes his hands over eyes in same gesture which drew sighs from the men before. There is absolute silence as the men watch the arisen corpses. Then, silently, a corpse rises in the middle of the trench, next to the* FIRST SOLDIER. *The* FIRST SOLDIER *screams, scrambles out of the trench in rear, and stands, bent over, watching the trench, middle-rear. There is no sound save the very light rumble of the guns. One by one the* CORPSES *arise and stand silently in their places, facing the rear, their backs to the audience. The* SOLDIERS *don't move, scarcely*

breathe, as, one by one, the CORPSES *appear.*
They stand there, a frozen tableau. Suddenly,
the SERGEANT *talks.)*

SERGEANT

What do you want?

FIRST CORPSE

Don't bury us.

THIRD SOLDIER

Let's get the hell out of here!

SERGEANT

(*Drawing pistol*)

Stay where you are! I'll shoot the first man that
moves

FIRST CORPSE

Don't bury us. We don't want to be buried.

SERGEANT

Christ! (*To men*) Carry on! (*The men stand
still*) Christ! (*The* SERGEANT *rushes off, calling*) Captain! Captain! Where the hell is the
Captain? (*His voice fades, te ror-stricken. The*
SOLDIERS *watch the* CORPSES, *then slowly, all together, start to back off.*)

SIXTH CORPSE

Don't go away.

SECOND CORPSE

Stay with us.

THIRD CORPSE

We want to hear the sound of men talking.

SIXTH CORPSE

Don't be afraid of us.

FIRST CORPSE

We're not really different from you. We're dead.

SECOND CORPSE

That's all...?

FOURTH CORPSE

All—all...

FIRST SOLDIER

That's all...?

THIRD CORPSE

Are you afraid of six dead men? You, who've lived with the dead, the so-many dead, and eaten your bread by their side when there was no time to bury them and you were hungry?

SECOND CORPSE

Are we different from you? An ounce or so of lead in our hearts, and none in yours. A small difference between us.

THIRD CORPSE

Tomorrow or the next day, the lead will be yours, too. Talk as our equals.

FOURTH SOLDIER

It's the kid—the one who wrote the dirty poems.

FIRST CORPSE

Say something to us. Forget the grave, as we would forget it....

THIRD SOLDIER

Do you—do you want a cigarette? (SERGEANT *re-enters with* CAPTAIN.)

SERGEANT

I'm not drunk! I'm not crazy, either! They just —got up, all together—and looked at us.... Look—look for yourself, Captain! (*The* CAPTAIN *stands off to one side, looking. The men stand at attention.*)

SERGEANT

See?

CAPTAIN

I see. (*He laughs sadly*) I was expecting it to happen—some day. So many men each day. It's too bad it had to happen in my company. Gentlemen! At ease! (*The men stand at ease. The* CAPTAIN *leaves. The guns roar suddenly. Fade-out.*)

The spotlight is turned on to the lower stage, right, below the platform on which the action, until now, has taken place. Discovered in its glare are three GENERALS, *around a table. The* CAPTAIN *is standing before them, talking.*

CAPTAIN

I'm only telling the Generals what I saw.

FIRST GENERAL

You're not making this up, Captain?

CAPTAIN

No, General.

SECOND GENERAL

Have you any proof, Captain?

CAPTAIN

The four men in the burial detail and the Sergeant, Sir.

THIRD GENERAL

In time of war, Captain, men see strange things.

CAPTAIN

Yes, General.

SECOND GENERAL

You've been drinking, Captain.

CAPTAIN

Yes, General.

SECOND GENERAL

When a man has been drinking, he is not responsible for what he sees.

CAPTAIN

Yes, General. I am not responsible for what I saw. I am glad of that. I would not like to carry that burden, along with all the others. . . .

FIRST GENERAL

Come, come, Captain, confess now. You were drinking and you walked out into the cold air over a field just lately won and what with the liquor and the air and the flush of victory . . .

CAPTAIN

I told the General what I saw.

SECOND GENERAL

Yes, we heard. We forgive you for it. We don't think any the worse of you for taking a nip. It's only natural. We understand. So take another drink with us now and forget your ghosts. . . .

CAPTAIN

They weren't ghosts. They were men—killed two days, standing in their graves and looking at me.

FIRST GENERAL

Captain, you're becoming trying. . . .

CAPTAIN

I'm sorry, Sir. It was a trying sight. I saw them and what are the Generals going to do about it?

SECOND GENERAL

Forget it! A man is taken for dead and put in a grave. He wakes from his coma and stands up. It happens every day—you've got to expect such things in a war. Take him out and send him to a hospital!

CAPTAIN

Hospitals aren't for dead men. What are the Generals going to do about them?

THIRD GENERAL

Don't stand there croaking, "What are the Generals going to do about them?" Have 'em examined by a doctor. If they're alive send them to a hospital. If they're dead, bury them! It's very simple.

CAPTAIN

But . . .

THIRD GENERAL

No buts, Sir!

CAPTAIN

Yes, Sir.

THIRD GENERAL

Take a doctor down with you, Sir, and a stenographer. Have the doctor dictate official reports. Have them witnessed. And let's hear no more of it.

CAPTAIN

Yes, Sir. Very good, Sir. (*Wheels to go out.*)

SECOND GENERAL

Oh, and Captain . . .

CAPTAIN

(*Stopping*)

Yes, Sir.

SECOND GENERAL

Stay away from the bottle.

CAPTAIN

Yes, Sir. Is that all, Sir?

SECOND GENERAL

That's all.

CAPTAIN

Yes, Sir. (*The light fades from the* GENERALS. *It follows the* CAPTAIN *as he walks across stage. The* CAPTAIN *stops, takes out a bottle. Takes two long swigs. Blackout.*)

The guns rumble, growing louder. They have been almost mute during GENERALS' *scene. The light is thrown on the burial scene again, where the* DOCTOR *is seen examining the* CORPSES *in their graves. The* DOCTOR *is armed with a stethoscope and is followed by a soldier stenographer, two of the* SOLDIERS, *impressed as witnesses, and the* CAPTAIN. *The* DOCTOR *is talking, as he passes from the first man.*

DOCTOR

Number one. Evisceration of the lower intestine. Dead forty-eight hours.

STENOGRAPHER
(*Repeating*)

Number one. Evisceration of the lower intestine.

Dead forty-eight hours. (*To witnesses*) Sign
here. (*They sign.*)

DOCTOR
(*On the next man*)
Number two. Bullet penetrated the left ven-
tricle. Dead forty-eight hours.

STENOGRAPHER
Number two. Bullet penetrated the left ven-
tricle. Dead forty-eight hours. (*To witnesses*)
Sign here. (*They sign.*)

DOCTOR
(*On the next* CORPSE)
Number three. Bullets penetrated both lungs.
Severe hemorrhages. Dead forty-eight hours.

STENOGRAPHER
(*Chanting*)
Number three. Bullets penetrated both lungs.
Severe hemorrhages. Dead forty-eight hours.
Sign here. (*The witnesses sign.*)

DOCTOR
(*On next* CORPSE)
Number four. Fracture of the skull and avulsion
of the cerebellum. Dead forty-eight hours.

STENOGRAPHER
Number four. Fracture of the skull and avul-
sion of the cerebellum. Dead forty-eight hours.
Sign here. (*The witnesses sign.*)

DOCTOR

(*Moving on to next* CORPSE)

Number five. Destruction of the genito-urinary system by shell-splinters. Death from hemorrhages. Dead forty-eight hours. Ummn. (*Looks curiously at* CORPSE'S *face*) Hum ... (*Moves on.*)

STENOGRAPHER

Number five. Destruction of the genito-urinary system by shell-splinters. Death from hemorrhages. Dead forty-eight hours. Sign here. (*The witnesses sign.*)

DOCTOR

(*On the next* CORPSE)

Number six. Destruction of right side of head from supra-orbital ridges through jaw-bone. Hum. You'd be a pretty sight for your mother, you would. Dead forty-eight hours ...

STENOGRAPHER

Number six. Destruction of right side of head from supra-orbital ridges through jaw-bone. You'd be a pretty sight for your mother, you would. Dead forty-eight hours. Sign here.

DOCTOR

What are you doing there?

STENOGRAPHER

That's what you said, Sir. . . .

DOCTOR

I know. Leave out—"You'd be a pretty sight for your mother, you would . . ." The Generals wouldn't be interested in that.

STENOGRAPHER

Yes, Sir. Sign here. (*The witnesses sign.*)

DOCTOR

Six, is that all?

CAPTAIN

Yes, Doctor. They're all dead?
(*The* FOURTH CORPSE *offers the* THIRD SOLDIER *a cigarette. The* THIRD SOLDIER *hesitates a second before taking it, then accepts it with a half-grin.*)

THIRD SOLDIER

Thanks, Buddy. I—I'm awful sorry—I— Thanks . . . (*He saves cigarette.*)

DOCTOR

(*Eyes on* FOURTH CORPSE *and* THIRD SOLDIER)
All dead.

CAPTAIN

A drink, Doctor?

DOCTOR

Yes, thank you. (*He takes the proffered bottle. Drinks long from it. Holds it, puts stethoscope in pocket with other hand. Stands looking at the* CORPSES, *lined up, facing the rear, nods, then*

takes another long drink. Silently hands bottle
to CAPTAIN, *who looks around him from one*
CORPSE *to another, then takes a long drink.*
Blackout.)

> *Spotlight on the* GENERALS, *facing the*
> CAPTAIN *and the* DOCTOR. *The* FIRST
> GENERAL *has the* DOCTOR'S *reports in his*
> *hands.*

FIRST GENERAL

Doctor!

DOCTOR

Yes, Sir.

FIRST GENERAL

In your reports here you say that each of these
six men is dead.

DOCTOR

Yes, Sir.

FIRST GENERAL

Then I don't see what all the fuss is about,
Captain. They're dead—bury them. . . .

CAPTAIN

I am afraid, Sir, that that can't be done. . . .
They are standing in their graves. They refuse
to be buried.

THIRD GENERAL

Do we have to go into that again? We have the

doctor's report. They're dead. Aren't they, Doctor?

DOCTOR

Yes, Sir.

THIRD GENERAL

Then they aren't standing in their graves, refusing to be buried, are they?

DOCTOR

Yes, Sir.

SECOND GENERAL

Doctor, would you know a dead man if you saw one?

DOCTOR

The symptoms are easily recognized.

FIRST GENERAL

You've been drinking, too. . . .

DOCTOR

Yes, Sir.

FIRST GENERAL

The whole damned army is drunk! I want a regulation announced tomorrow morning in all regiments. No more liquor is to be allowed within twenty miles of the front line upon pain of death. Got it?

SECOND GENERAL

Yes, General. But then how'll we get the men to fight?

FIRST GENERAL

Damn the fighting! We can't have stories like this springing up. It's bad for the morale! Did you hear me, Doctor, it's bad for the morale and you ought to be ashamed of yourself!

DOCTOR

Yes, Sir.

THIRD GENERAL

This has gone far enough. If it goes any farther, the men will get wind of it. We have witnessed certificates from a registered surgeon that these men are dead. Bury them! Waste no more time on it. Did you hear me, Captain?

CAPTAIN

Yes, Sir. I'm afraid, Sir, that I must refuse to bury these men.

THIRD GENERAL

That's insubordination, Sir. . . .

CAPTAIN

I'm sorry, Sir. It is not within the line of my military duties to bury men against their will. If the General will only think for a moment he will see that this is impossible. . . .

FIRST GENERAL

The Captain's right. It might get back to Congress. God only knows what *they'd* make of it!

THIRD GENERAL

What are we going to do then?

FIRST GENERAL

Captain, what do you suggest?

CAPTAIN

Stop the war.

CHORUS OF GENERALS

Captain!

FIRST GENERAL
(*With great dignity*)

Captain, we beg of you to remember the gravity of the situation. It admits of no levity. Is that the best suggestion you can make, Captain?

CAPTAIN

Yes. But I have another— If the Generals would come down to the grave themselves and attempt to influence these—ah—corpses—to lie down, perhaps that would prove effective. We're seven miles behind the line now and we could screen the roads to protect your arrival. . . .

FIRST GENERAL
(*Coughing*)

Umm—uh—usually, of course, that would be —uh . . . We'll see. In the meantime it must be kept quiet! Remember that! Not a word! Nobody must know! God only knows what would happen if people began to suspect we couldn't even get our dead to lie down and be buried! This is the god-damndest war! They never said anything about this sort of thing at West Point. Remember, not a word, nobody must know, quiet as the grave, *mum! ssssh!* (*All the* GENERALS *repeat the ssssh after him.*)

The light fades—but the hiss of the GENERALS *hushing each other is still heard as the light falls on another part of the stage proper, where two soldiers are on post in the front lines, behind a barricade of sandbags. The sound of guns is very strong. There are flashes of gun-fire.*

BEVINS

(*A soldier past forty, fat, with a pot-belly and graying hair showing under his helmet*)

Did you hear about those guys that won't let themselves be buried, Charley?

CHARLEY

I heard. You never know what's gonna happen next in this lousy war.

BEVINS

What do you think about it, Charley?

CHARLEY

What're they gettin' out of it, that's what I'd like to know. They're just makin' things harder.

I heard all about 'em. They stink! Bury 'em.
That's what I say.

CHARLEY

BEVINS

I don't know, Charley. I kinda can see what
they're aimin' at. Christ, I wouldn't like to be
put six foot under now, I wouldn't. What the
hell for?

CHARLEY

What's the difference?

BEVINS

There's a difference, all right. It's kinda good,
bein' alive. It's kinda nice, bein' on top of the
earth and seein' things and hearin' things and
smellin' things. . . .

CHARLEY

Yeah, smellin' stiffs that ain't had time to be
buried. That sure is sweet.

BEVINS

Yeah, but it's better than havin' the dirt packed
onto your face. I guess those guys felt sorta
gypped when they started throwin' the dirt in
on 'em and they just couldn't stand it, dead
or no dead.

CHARLEY

They're dead, ain't they? Nobody's puttin' them
under while they're alive

BEVINS

It amounts to the same thing, Charley. They should be alive now. What are they—a parcel of kids? Kids shouldn't be dead, Charley. That's what they musta figured when the dirt started fallin' in on 'em. What the hell are they doin' dead? Did they get anything out of it? Did anybody ask them? Did they want to be standin' there when the lead poured in? They're just kids, or guys with wives and young kids of their own. They wanted to be home readin' a book or teachin' their kid c-a-t spells cat or takin' a woman out into the country in a open car with the wind blowin'.... That's the way it musta come to them, when the dirt smacked on their faces, dead or no dead....

CHARLEY

Bury them. That's what I say.... (*There is the chatter of a machine gun off in the night.* BEVINS *is hit. He staggers.*)

BEVINS

(*Clutching his throat*)
Charley—Charley... (*His fingers bring down the top sandbag as he falls. The machine gun chatters again and* CHARLEY *is hit. He staggers.*)

CHARLEY

Oh, my God... (*The machine gun chatters again. He falls over* BEVINS. *There is quiet for a moment. Then the eternal artillery again. Blackout.*)

> *A baby spotlight, white, picks out the* FIRST GENERAL, *standing over the prone forms of the two soldiers. He has his fingers to his lips.*

FIRST GENERAL
(*In a hoarse whisper*)

Sssh! Keep it quiet! Nobody must know! Not a word! Sssh! (*Blackout.*)

> *A spotlight picks out another part of the stage—a newspaper office.* EDITOR *at his desk,* REPORTER *before him, hat on head.*

REPORTER

That's the story! It's as straight as a rifle-barrel, so help me God.

EDITOR
(*Looking down at manuscript in hand*)

This is a freak, all right. I never came across anything like it in all the years I've been putting out a newspaper.

REPORTER

There never was anything like it before. It's somethin' new. Somethin's happening. Somebody's waking up. . . .

EDITOR

It didn't happen.

REPORTER

So help me God, I got it straight. Those guys just stood up in the grave and said, "The hell with it, you can't bury us!" God's honest truth.

EDITOR

(*Picks up telephone*)
Get me Macready at the War Department.... It's an awfully funny story....

REPORTER

What about it? It's the story of the year—the story of the century—the biggest story of all time—men gettin' up with bullets in their hearts and refusin' to be buried....

EDITOR

Who do they think they are—Jesus Christ?

REPORTER

What's the difference? That's the story! You can't miss it! You goin' to put it in? Lissen—are you goin' to put it in?

EDITOR

Hold it! (*Into telephone*) Macready!

REPORTER

What's he got to do with it?

EDITOR

I'll find out. What are *you* so hot about? ... Hello! Macready? Hansen from the New York...

Yeah.... Listen, Macready, I got this story about the six guys who refuse to be... Yeah....

REPORTER

What does he say?

EDITOR

Okay, Macready. Yeah, if that's the way the Government feels about it.... Yeah....

REPORTER

Well?

EDITOR

(*Putting down telephone*)

No.

REPORTER

Holy god-damn, you got to. People got a right to know.

EDITOR

In time of war, people have a right to know nothing. If we put it in, it'd be censored anyway.

REPORTER

Ah, this is a lousy business. . . .

EDITOR

Write another human interest story about the boys at the front. That'll keep you busy. You know...that one about how the boys in the front-line sing "I Can't Give You Anything but Love," before they go over the top....

REPORTER

But I wrote that last week.

EDITOR

It made a great hit. Write it again.

REPORTER

But these guys in the grave, Boss. Lloyds are giving three to one they won't go down. That's a story!

EDITOR

Save it. You can write a book of memoirs twenty years from now. Make that "I Can't Give You Anything but Love" story a thousand words, and make it snappy. The casualty lists run into two pages today and we got to balance them with something....

(*Blackout*)

> *Rumble of guns. The spotlight illuminates the grave on the platform, where the* CORPSES *are still standing, hip-deep, facing the rear. The burial squad is there, and the* CAPTAIN, *and the* GENERALS.

CAPTAIN

There they are. What are the Generals going to do about them?

FIRST GENERAL
(*Pettishly*)

I see them. Stop saying "What are the Generals going to do about them?"

SECOND GENERAL

Who do they think they are?

THIRD GENERAL

It's against all regulations.

FIRST GENERAL

Quiet, please, quiet. Let's not have any scenes.
... This must be handled with authority—but
tactfully. I'll talk to them! (*He goes over to
brink of grave*) Men! Listen to me! This is a
strange situation in which we find ourselves. I
have no doubt but that it is giving you as much
embarrassment as it is us. ...

SECOND GENERAL

(*Confidentially to* THIRD GENERAL)

The wrong note. He's good on artillery, but
when it comes to using his head, he's lost. ...
He's been that way ever since I knew him.

FIRST GENERAL

We're all anxious to get this thing over with
just as quickly and quietly as possible. I know
that you men are with me on this. There's no
reason why we can't get together and settle this
in jig time. I grant, my friends, that it's unfor-
tunate that you're dead. I'm sure that you'll all
listen to reason. Listen, too, to the voice of duty,
the voice that sent you here to die bravely for
your country. Gentlemen, your country demands

of you that you lie down and allow yourselves to be buried. Must our flag fly at half-mast and droop in the wind while you so far forget your duty to the lovely land that bore and nurtured you? I love America, gentlemen, its hills and valleys. If you loved America as I do, you would not ... (*He breaks down, overcome*) I find it difficult to go on. (*He pauses*) I have studied this matter and come to the conclusion that the best thing for all concerned would be for you men to lie down peaceably in your graves and allow yourselves to be buried. (*He waits. The* CORPSES *do not move.*)

THIRD GENERAL

It didn't work. He's not firm enough. You've got to be firm right from the beginning or you're lost.

FIRST GENERAL

Men, perhaps you don't understand. (*To* CORPSES) I advise you to allow yourselves to be buried. (*They stand, motionless*) You're dead, men, don't you realize that? You can't be dead and stand there like that. Here ... here ... I'll prove it to you! (*He gets out* DOCTOR's *reports*) Look! A doctor's reports. Witnessed! Witnessed by Privates McGurk and Butler. (*He reads the names*) This ought to show you! (*He *waves the reports. He stands on the brink of the grave, middle-rear, glaring at the* CORPSES. *He shouts at them*) You're dead, officially, all of you! I won't mince words! You heard! We're a civilized race, we bury our dead. Lie down! (*The* CORPSES *stand*) Private Driscoll! Private Schelling! Private Morgan! Private Levy! Private Webster! Private Dean! Lie down! As Commander-in-Chief of the Army as appointed by the President of the United States in accordance with the Constitution of the United States, and as your superior officer, I command you to lie down and allow yourselves to be buried. (*They stand, silent and motionless*) Tell me— What is it going to get you, staying above the earth? (*Not a sound from the* CORPSES) I asked you a question, men. Answer me! What is it going to get you? If I were dead I wouldn't hesitate to be buried. Answer me...what do you want? What is it going to get you...(*As they remain silent*) Tell me! Answer me! Why don't you talk? Explain it to me, make me understand...

SECOND GENERAL

(*In whisper to* THIRD GENERAL, *as* FIRST GENERAL *glares hopelessly at the* CORPSES)

He's licked. It was a mistake—moving him off the artillery.

THIRD GENERAL

They ought to let me handle them. I'd show 'em. You've got to use force.

FIRST GENERAL

(*Bursting out—after walking along entire row of* CORPSES *and back*)
Lie down! (*The* CORPSES *stand, immobile. The* GENERAL *rushes out, moaning*) Oh, God, oh, my God . . . (*Blackout.*)

Spotlight, red, picks out two WHORES, *dressed in the uniform of their trade, on a street corner.*

FIRST WHORE

I'd lay 'em, all right. They oughta call me in. I'd lay 'em. There wouldn't be any doubt in anybody's mind after I got through with 'em. Why don't they call me in instead of those Generals? What do Generals know about such things? (*Both* WHORES *go off into fits of wild laughter*) Call the War Department, Mabel, tell 'em we'll come to their rescue at the prevailing rates. (*Laugh wildly again*) We're willing to do our part, like the papers say—share the burden! Oh, my Gawd, I ain't laughed so much . . . (*Laugh again. A* MAN *crosses their path. Still laughing, but professional*) Say, Johnny, Johnny, what'cha doin' tonight? How'd

ya like . . . ? (*The* MAN *passes on. The women
laugh*) Share the burden—Oh, my Gawd . . .
(*They laugh and laugh and laugh, clinging to
each other. . . . Blackout. But the laughter goes
on.*)

> *The spotlight illuminates the grave—*
> SOLDIERS *of burial detail are sitting around
> a covered fire.* SECOND SOLDIER *is singing
> "Swing Low, Sweet Chariot."*

THIRD SOLDIER

This is a funny war. It's rollin' downhill. Everybody's waitin'. Personally, I think it's those guys
there that . . . (*He gestures to grave.*)

SERGEANT

Nobody asked you. You're not supposed to talk
about it.

FIRST SOLDIER

Regulation 2035a . . .

SERGEANT

Well, I just told ya. (SECOND SOLDIER *starts to
sing again.* SERGEANT *breaks in on him*) Say,
lissen, think about those guys there. How do
you think they feel with you howlin' like this?
They got more important things to think about.

SECOND SOLDIER

I won't distract 'em. I got an easy-flowin' voice.

SERGEANT

They don't like it. I can tell.

FIRST SOLDIER

Well, *I* like to hear him sing. And I'll bet they do, too. I'm gonna ask 'em ... (*He jumps up.*)

SERGEANT

Now, lissen! (FIRST SOLDIER *slowly approaches the grave. He is embarrassed, a little frightened.*)

FIRST SOLDIER

Say, men, I ... (CAPTAIN *comes on.* FIRST SOLDIER *stands at attention.*)

CAPTAIN

Sergeant ...

SERGEANT

Yes, Sir!

CAPTAIN

You know that none of the men is to talk to *them.* ...

SERGEANT

Yes, Sir. Only, Sir ...

CAPTAIN

All right. (*To* FIRST SOLDIER) Get back there, please.

FIRST SOLDIER

Yes, Sir! (*He salutes and goes back.*)

SERGEANT

(*Under his breath to* FIRST SOLDIER) I warned
ya.

FIRST SOLDIER

Shut up! I wanna lissen to what's goin' on there!
(CAPTAIN *has meanwhile seated himself on the
edge of the grave and has brought out a pair
of eyeglasses with which he plays as he talks.*)

CAPTAIN

Gentlemen, I have been asked by the Generals
to talk to you. My work is not this... (*He
indicates his uniform*) I am a philosopher, a
scientist, my uniform is a pair of eye-glasses, my
usual weapons test-tubes and books. At a time
like this perhaps we need philosophy, need
science. First I must say that your General has
ordered you to lie down.

FIRST CORPSE

We used to have a General.

THIRD CORPSE

No more.

FOURTH CORPSE

They sold us.

CAPTAIN

What do you mean—sold you!

FIFTH CORPSE

Sold us for twenty-five yards of bloody mud.

SIXTH CORPSE

A life for four yards of bloody mud.

CAPTAIN

We had to take that hill. General's orders.
You're soldiers. You understand.

FIRST CORPSE

We understand now. The real estate operations
of Generals are always carried on at boom
prices.

SIXTH CORPSE

A life for four yards of bloody mud. Gold is
cheaper, and rare jewels, pearls and rubies. . . .

THIRD CORPSE

I fell in the first yard. . . .

SECOND CORPSE

I caught on the wire and hung there while the
machine gun stitched me through the middle
to it. . . .

FOURTH CORPSE

I was there at the end and thought I had life in
my hands for another day, but a shell came and
my life dripped into the mud.

SIXTH CORPSE

Ask the General how he'd like to be dead at
twenty. (*Calling, as though to the* GENERALS)
Twenty, General, twenty . . .

CAPTAIN

Other men are dead.

FIRST CORPSE

Too many.

CAPTAIN

Men must die for their country's sake—if not you, then others. This has always been. Men died for Pharaoh and Cæsar and Rome two thousand years ago and more, and went into the earth with their wounds. Why not you...?

FIRST CORPSE

Men, even the men who die for Pharaoh and Cæsar and Rome, must, in the end, before all hope is gone, discover that a man can die happy and be contentedly buried only when he dies for himself or for a cause that is his own and not Pharaoh's or Cæsar's or Rome's....

CAPTAIN

Still—what is this world, that you cling to it? A speck of dust, a flaw in the skies, a thumb-print on the margin of a page printed in an incomprehensible language....

SECOND CORPSE

It is our home.

THIRD CORPSE

We have been dispossessed by force, but we are reclaiming our home. It is time that mankind claimed its home—this earth—its home....

CAPTAIN

We have no home. We are strangers in the universe and cling, desperate and grimy, to the crust of our world, and if there is a God and this His earth, we must be a terrible sight in His eyes.

FOURTH CORPSE

We are not disturbed by the notion of our appearance in the eyes of God....

CAPTAIN

The earth is an unpleasant place and when you are rid of it you are well rid of it. Man cheats man here and the only sure things are death and despair. Of what use, then, to remain on it once you have the permission to leave?

FIFTH CORPSE

It is the one thing we know.

SIXTH CORPSE

We did not ask permission to leave. Nobody asked us whether we wanted it or not. The Generals pushed us out and closed the door on us. Who are the Generals that they are to close doors on us?

CAPTAIN

The earth, I assure you, is a mean place, insignificantly miserable....

FIRST CORPSE

We must find out for ourselves. That is our right.

CAPTAIN

Man has no rights. . . .

FIRST CORPSE

Man can make rights for himself. It requires
only determination and the good-will of ordi-
nary men. We have made ourselves the right to
walk this earth, seeing it and judging it for ourselves.

CAPTAIN

There is peace in the grave. . . .

THIRD CORPSE

Peace and the worms and the roots of grass.
There is a deeper peace than that which comes
with feeding the roots of the grass.

CAPTAIN

(*Looks slowly at them, in turn*) Yes, gentlemen . . . (*Turns away and walks off.* FIRST
SOLDIER *moves slowly up to the grave.*)

FIRST SOLDIER

(*To the* CORPSES) I . . . I'm glad you . . . you
didn't . . . I'm glad. Say, is there anything we
can do for you?

SERGEANT

Lissen, soldier!

FIRST SOLDIER

(*Passionately, harshly*) Shut up, Sergeant!
(*Then very softly and warmly to* FIRST CORPSE)
Is there anything we can do for you, Friend?

FIRST CORPSE

Yeah. You can sing... (*There is a pause in which the* FIRST SOLDIER *turns around and looks at the* SECOND SOLDIER, *then back to the* FIRST CORPSE. *Then the silence is broken by the* SECOND SOLDIER'S *voice, raised in song. It goes on for a few moments, then fades as the light dims.*)

> *Colored spotlights pick out three* BUSINESS MEN *on different parts of the stage.*

FIRST BUSINESS MAN

Ssh! Keep it quiet!

THIRD BUSINESS MAN

Sink 'em with lead....

SECOND BUSINESS MAN

Bury them! Bury them six feet under!

FIRST BUSINESS MAN

What are we going to do?

SECOND BUSINESS MAN

We must keep up the morale.

THIRD BUSINESS MAN

Lead! Lead! A lot of lead!

SECOND BUSINESS MAN

What do we pay our Generals for?

CHORUS OF BUSINESS MEN
Ssssh!
(*Blackout*)

Spotlight on the congregation of a church, kneeling, with a PRIEST *praying over them.*

PRIEST

O Jesus, our God and our Christ, Who has re-deemed us with Thy blood on the Cross at Calvary, give us Thy blessing on this holy day, and cause it that our soldiers allow themselves to be buried in peace, and bring victory to our arms, enlisted in Thy Cause and the cause of all righteousness on the field of battle... Amen ... (*Blackout.*)

FIRST GENERAL
(*In purple baby spotlight*)
Please, God, keep it quiet...

(*Spotlight on newspaper office.*)

REPORTER
Well? What are you going to do?

EDITOR
Do I have to do anything?

REPORTER

God damn right you do. . . . They're still standing up. They're going to stand up from now till
Doomsday. They're not going to be able to bury
soldiers any more. It's in the stars. . . . You got
to say something about it. . . .

EDITOR

All right. Put this in. "It is alleged that certain
members of an infantry regiment refuse to allow themselves to be buried. . . ."

REPORTER

Well?

EDITOR

That's all.

REPORTER
(*Incredulous*)

That's all?

EDITOR

Yes, Christ, isn't that *enough*? (*Blackout.*)

Spotlight on a radio-loudspeaker. A VOICE,
mellow and beautiful, comes out of it.

THE VOICE

It has been reported that certain American
soldiers, killed on the field of battle, have re-
fused to allow themselves to be buried.
Whether this is true or not, the Coast-to-Coast

Broadcasting System feels that this must give
the American public an idea of the indomitable
spirit of the American doughboy in this war.
We cannot rest until this war is won—not even
our brave dead boys... (*Blackout.*)

> *Guns. Spotlight on* FIRST GENERAL *and*
> CAPTAIN.

FIRST GENERAL

Have you got any suggestions...?

CAPTAIN

I think so. Get their women....

FIRST GENERAL

What good'll their women do?

CAPTAIN

Women are always conservative. It's a conservative notion—this one of lying down and
allowing yourself to be buried when you're
dead. The women'll fight the General's battle for
them—in the best possible way—through their
emotions.... It's the General's best bet....

FIRST GENERAL

Women— Of course! You've got it there, Captain! Get out their women! Get them in a
hurry! We'll have these boys underground in
a jiffy. Women! By God, I never thought of it.
... Send out the call.... Women! (*Fadeout.*)

A baby spotlight on the loudspeaker. The VOICE *again, just as mellow, just as persuasive.*

VOICE

We have been asked by the War Department to broadcast an appeal to the women of Privates Driscoll, Schelling, Morgan, Webster, Levy, and Dean, reported dead. The War Department requests that the women of these men present themselves at the War Department Office immediately. It is within their power to do a great service to their country.... (*Blackout.*)

The spotlight illuminates the FIRST GENERAL, *where he stands, addressing six women.*

FIRST GENERAL

Go to your men ... talk to them ... make them see the error of their ways, ladies. You women represent what is dearest in our civilization—the sacred foundations of the home. We are fighting this war to protect the foundations of the homes of America! Those foundations will crumble utterly if these men of yours come back from the dead. I shudder to think of the consequences of such an act. Our entire system will be mortally struck. Our banks will close, our buildings collapse ... our army will desert the field and leave our fair land open to be overrun by the enemy. Ladies, you are all Gold Star mothers and wives and sweethearts. You want to win this war. I know it. I know the high fire of patriotism that burns in women's breasts. That is why I have called upon you. Ladies, let me make this clear to you. If you do not get your men to lie down and allow themselves to be buried, I fear that our cause is lost. The burden of the war is upon your shoulders now. Wars are not fought with guns and powder alone, ladies. Here is your chance to do your part, a glorious part. ... You are fighting for your homes, your children, your sisters' lives, your country's honor. You are fighting for religion, for love, for all decent human life. Wars can be fought and won only when the dead are buried and forgotten. How can we forget the dead who refuse to be buried? And we *must* forget them! There is no room in this world for dead men. They will lead only to the bitterest unhappiness—for you, for them, for everybody. Go, ladies, do your duty. Your country waits upon you. ... (*Blackout.*)

Spotlight immediately illuminates the place where PRIVATE SCHELLING, CORPSE

TWO, is talking to his wife. MRS. SCHELLING *is a spare, taciturn woman, a farmer's wife, who might be twenty or forty or anything in between.*

BESS SCHELLING

Did it hurt much, John?

SCHELLING

How's the kid, Bess?

BESS

He's fine. He talks now. He weighs twenty-eight pounds. He'll be a big boy. Did it hurt much, John?

SCHELLING

How is the farm? Is it going all right, Bess?

BESS

It's going. The rye was heavy this year. Did it hurt much, John?

SCHELLING

Who did the reapin' for you, Bess?

BESS

Schmidt took care of it—and his boys. Schmidt's too old for the war and his boys are too young. Took 'em nearly two weeks. The wheat's not bad this year. Schmidt's oldest boy expects to be called in a month or two. He practises behind the barn with that old shotgun Schmidt uses for duck.

SCHELLING

The Schmidts were always fools. When the kid grows up, Bess, you make sure you pump some sense into his head. What color's his hair?

BESS

Blond. Like you. . . . What are you going to do, John?

SCHELLING

I would like to see the kid—and the farm— and . . .

BESS

They say you're dead, John. . . .

SCHELLING

I'm dead, all right.

BESS

Then how is it . . . ?

SCHELLING

I don't know. Maybe there's too many of us under the ground now. Maybe the earth can't stand it no more. You got to change crops sometime. What are you doing here, Bess?

BESS

They asked me to get you to let yourself be buried.

SCHELLING

What do you think?

BESS

You're dead, John. . . .

SCHELLING

Well . . . ?

BESS

What's the good . . . ?

SCHELLING

I don't know. Only there's something in me, dead or no dead, that won't let me be buried.

BESS

You were a queer man, John. I never did understand what you were about. But what's the good . . . ?

SCHELLING

Bess, I never talked so that I could get you to understand what I wanted while I—while I—before . . . Maybe now . . . There're a couple of things, Bess, that I ain't had enough of. Easy things, the things you see when you look outa your window at night, after supper, or when you wake up in the mornin'. Things you smell when you step outside the door when summer's on and the sun starts to turn the grass brown. Things you hear when you're busy with the horses or pitchin' the hay and you don't really notice them and yet they come back to you. Things like the fuzz of green over a field in spring where you planted wheat and it's started to come out overnight. Things like lookin' at rows of corn scrapin' in the breeze, tall and green, with the silk flying off the ears in the wind. Things like seeing the sweat come out all over on your horse's fat flank and seein' it shine like silk in front of you, smelling horsey and strong. Things like seein' the loam turn back all fat and deep brown on both sides as the plough turns it over so that it gets to be awful hard walkin' behind it. Things like taking a cold drink of water outa the well after you've boiled in the sun all afternoon, and feelin' the water go down and down into you coolin' you off all through from the inside out.... Things like seein' a blond kid, all busy and serious, playin' with a dog on the shady side of a house.... There ain't nothin' like that down here, Bess....

BESS

Everything has its place, John. Dead men have theirs.

SCHELLING

My place is on the earth, Bess. My business is with the top of the earth, not the under-side. It was a trap that yanked me down. I'm not smart, Bess, and I'm easy trapped—but I can tell now ... I got some stories to tell farmers before I'm through—I'm going to tell 'em....

BESS

We could bury you home, John, near the creek

—it's cool there and quiet and there's always a breeze in the trees. . . .

SCHELLING

Later, Bess, when I've had my fill of lookin' and smellin' and talkin'. . . . A man should be able to walk into his grave, not be dragged into it. . . .

BESS

How'll I feel—and the kid—with you walkin' around—like—like that . . . ?

SCHELLING

I won't bother you. . . . I won't come near you. . . .

BESS

Even so. Just knowin' . . .

SCHELLING

I can't help it. This is somethin' bigger'n you—bigger'n me. It's somethin' I ain't had nothin' to do with startin'. . . . It's somethin' that just grew up outa the earth—like—like a weed—a flower. Cut it down now and it'll jump up in a dozen new places. You can't stop it. The earth's ready for it. . . .

BESS

You were a good husband, John. For the kid—and me—won't you?

SCHELLING

(*Quietly*)

Go home, Bess. *Go home!* (*Blackout.*)

> *The spotlight picks out* CORPSE NUMBER
> FIVE, PRIVATE LEVY, *where he stands in
> the grave, with his back to the audience.
> His woman, a pert, attractive young lady,
> is sitting next to him, above him, facing
> him, talking to him.*

JOAN

You loved me best, didn't you, Henry—of all
of them—all those women—you loved me the
best, didn't you?

LEVY (FIFTH CORPSE)

What's the difference, now?

JOAN

I want to know it.

LEVY

It's not important.

JOAN

It's important to me. I knew about the others,
about Doris and that shifty-eyed Janet....
Henry, you're not a live man, are you, Henry?

LEVY

No, I'm all shot away inside.

JOAN

Must wars always be fought in the mud like this? I never expected it to look like this. It... it looks like a dump heap.

LEVY

You've gotten your shoes muddy. They're pretty shoes, Joan.

JOAN

Do you think so, Henry? They're lizard. I like them too. It's so hard to get a good pair of shoes nowadays.

LEVY

Do you still dance, Joan?

JOAN

Oh, I'm really much better than I used to be. There are so many dances back home nowadays. Dances for orphan relief and convalescent hospitals and Victory Loans. I'm busy seven nights a week. I sold more Victory Loans than any other girl in the League. I got a helmet... one of *their* helmets... one with a bullet-hole in it, for selling eleven thousand dollars' worth.

LEVY

Out here we get them for nothing, by the million —bullet-holes and all.

JOAN

That sounds bitter. You shouldn't sound bitter.

LEVY

I'm sorry.

JOAN

I heard Colonel Elwell the other day. You know Colonel Elwell, old Anthony Elwell who owns the mill. He made a speech at the monthly Red Cross banquet and he said that that was the nice thing about this war, it wasn't being fought bitterly by our boys. He said it was just patriotism that kept us going. He's a wonderful speaker, Colonel Elwell; I cried and cried....

LEVY

I remember him.

JOAN

Henry, do you think we're going to win the war?

LEVY

What's the difference?

JOAN

Henry! What a way to talk! I don't know what's come over you. Really, I don't. Why, the papers say that if *they* win the war, they'll burn our churches and tear down our museums and... and rape our women. (LEVY *laughs*) Why are you laughing, Henry?

LEVY

I'm dead, Joan.

JOAN

Yes. Then why—why don't you let them bury you?

LEVY

There are a lot of reasons. There were a lot of things I loved on this earth. . . .

JOAN

A dead man can't touch a woman.

LEVY

The women, yes—but more than touching them. I got a great joy just from listening to women, hearing them laugh, watching their skirts blow in the wind, noticing the way their breasts bounced up and down inside their dresses when they walked. It had nothing to do with touching them. I liked to hear the sound of their high heels on pavements at night and the tenderness in their voices when they walked past me arm in arm with a young man. You were so lovely, Joan, with your pale hair and long hands.

JOAN

You always liked my hair. (*A pause*) No woman will walk arm in arm with you, Henry Levy, while you cheat the grave.

LEVY

No. But there will be the eyes of women to look at and the bright color of their hair and the soft way they swing their hips when they walk before young men. These are the things that mean life and the earth to me, the joy and the pain. These are the things the earth still owes me, now when I am only thirty. Joy and pain—to each man in his own way, a full seventy years, to be ended by an unhurried fate, not by a colored pin on a General's map. What do I care for the colored pins on a General's map?

JOAN

They are not only pins. They mean more. . . .

LEVY

More? To whom? To the Generals—not to me. To me they are colored pins. It is not a fair bargain—this exchange of my life for a small part of a colored pin. . . .

JOAN

Henry, how can you talk like that? You know why this war is being fought.

LEVY

No. Do you?

JOAN

Of course, everybody knows. We *must* win! We must be prepared to sacrifice our last drop of blood. Anyway, what can you do?

LEVY

Do you remember last summer, Joan? My last leave. We went to Maine. I would like to re-

member that—the sun and the beach and your
soft hands—for a long time.

JOAN

What are you going to do?

LEVY

Walk the world looking at the fine, long-legged
girls, seeing in them something deep and true
and passionately vital, listening to the sound of
their light voices with ears the Generals would
have stopped with the grave's solid mud. . . .

JOAN

Henry! Henry! Once you said you loved me.
For love of me, Henry, go into the grave. . . .

LEVY

Poor Joan. (*Stretches out his hand tenderly as if
to touch her.*)

JOAN
(*Recoiling*)

Don't touch me. (*Pause*) For love of me.

LEVY

Go home, Joan! *Go home!* (*Blackout.*)

The spotlight picks out the THIRD CORPSE,
PRIVATE MORGAN, *and* JULIA BLAKE, *he
with his back to the audience, standing in
the grave, she above and to the right.*
JULIA *sobs.*

MORGAN

Stop crying, Julia. What's the sense in crying?

JULIA

No sense. Only I can't stop crying.

MORGAN

You shouldn't have come.

JULIA

They asked me to come. They said you wouldn't let them bury you—dead and all. . . .

MORGAN

Yes.

JULIA
(*Crying*)

Why don't they kill me too? I'd let them bury me. I'd be glad to be buried—to get away from all this . . . I—I haven't stopped crying for two weeks now. I used to think I was tough. I never cried. Even when I was a kid. It's a wonder where all the tears can come from. Though I guess there's always room for more tears. I thought I was all cried out when I heard about the way they killed Fred. My kid brother. I used to comb his hair in the morning when he went to school . . . I—I . . . Then they killed you. They did, didn't they?

MORGAN

Yes.

JULIA

It's hard to know like this. I—I know, though. It—it makes it harder, this way, with you like this. I could forget easier if you ... But I wasn't going to say that. I was going to listen to you. Oh, my darling, it's been so rotten. I get drunk. I hate it and I get drunk. I sing out loud and everybody laughs. I was going through your things the other day—I'm crazy ... I go through all your things three times a week, touching your clothes and reading your books. ... You have the nicest clothes. ... There was that quatrain you wrote to me that time you were in Boston and ... First I laughed, then I cried, then ... It's a lovely poem—you would have been a fine writer. I think you would have been the greatest writer that ever ... I ... Did they shoot your hands away, darling?

MORGAN

No.

JULIA

That's good. I couldn't bear it if anything happened to your hands. Was it bad, darling?

MORGAN

Bad enough.

JULIA

But they didn't shoot your hands away. That's something. You learn how to be grateful for the craziest things nowadays. People have to be grateful for something and it's so hard, with the war and all. . . . Oh, darling, I never could think of you dead. Somehow you didn't seem to be made to be dead. I would feel better if you were buried in a fine green field and there were funny little flowers jumping up around the stone that said, "Walter Morgan, Born 1913, Died 1937." I could stop getting drunk at night and singing out loud so that people laugh at me. The worst thing is looking at all the books you piled up home that you didn't read. They wait there, waiting for your hands to come and open them and . . . Oh, let them bury you, let them bury you . . . There's nothing left, only crazy people and clothes that'll never be used hanging in the closets . . . Why not?

MORGAN

There are too many books I haven't read, too many places I haven't seen, too many memories I haven't kept long enough. . . . I won't be cheated of them. . . .

JULIA

And me? Darling, me . . . I hate getting drunk. Your name would look so well on a nice simple chunk of marble in a green field. "Walter Morgan, Beloved of Julia Blake . . ." With poppies and daisies and those little purple flowers all around the bottom, and ... (*She is bent over, almost wailing. There is the flash of a gun in her hand, and she totters, falls*) Now they can put my name on the casualty lists, too. ... What do they call those purple flowers, darling ... ? (*Blackout.*)

The spotlight follows KATHERINE DRIS-COLL *as she makes her way from* CORPSE *to* CORPSE *in the grave, looking at their faces. She looks first at* CORPSE SIX, *shudders, covers her eyes and moves on. She stops at* CORPSE FIVE.

KATHERINE

I'm Katherine Driscoll. I—I'm looking for my brother. He's dead. Are you my brother?

FIFTH CORPSE

No. (KATHERINE *goes on to* CORPSE FOUR, *stops, looks, moves on to* CORPSE THREE.)

KATHERINE

I'm looking for my brother. My name is Katherine Driscoll. His name—

THIRD CORPSE

No. (KATHERINE *goes on, stands irresolutely before* CORPSE TWO.)

KATHERINE

Are you ... ? (*Realizing it isn't her brother.
Goes on to* CORPSE ONE) I'm looking for my
brother. My name is Katherine Driscoll. His
name—

DRISCOLL

I'm Tom Driscoll.

KATHERINE

Hel—Hello. I don't know you. After fifteen
years— And ...

DRISCOLL

What do you want, Katherine?

KATHERINE

You don't know me either, do you?

DRISCOLL

No.

KATHERINE

It's funny—my coming here to talk to a dead
man—to try to get him to do something because
once long ago he was my brother. They talked
me into it. I don't know how to begin. ...

DRISCOLL

You'll be wasting your words, Katherine. ...

KATHERINE

They should have asked someone nearer to you
—someone who loved you—only they couldn't
find anybody. I was the nearest, they said. ...

DRISCOLL

That's so. You were the nearest. . . .

KATHERINE

And I fifteen years away. Poor Tom... It couldn't have been a sweet life you led these fifteen years.

DRISCOLL

It wasn't.

KATHERINE

You were poor, too?

DRISCOLL

Sometimes I begged for meals. I wasn't lucky. . . .

KATHERINE

And yet you want to go back. Is there no more sense in the dead, Tom, than in the living?

DRISCOLL

Maybe not. Maybe there's no sense in either living or dying, but we can't believe that. I travelled to a lot of places and I saw a lot of things, always from the black side of them, always workin' hard to keep from starvin' and turnin' my collar up to keep the wind out, and they were mean and rotten and sad, but always I saw that they could be better and some day they were going to be better, and that the guys like me who knew that they were rotten and knew that they could be better had to get out and fight to make it that way.

KATHERINE

You're dead. Your fight's over.

DRISCOLL

The fight's never over. I got things to say to people now—to the people who nurse big machines and the people who swing shovels and the people whose babies die with big bellies and rotten bones. I got things to say to the people who leave their lives behind them and pick up guns to fight in somebody else's war. Important things. Big things. Big enough to lift me out of the grave right back onto the earth into the middle of men just because I got the voice to say them. If God could lift Jesus...

KATHERINE

Tom! Have you lost religion, too?

DRISCOLL

I got another religion. I got a religion that wants to take heaven out of the clouds and plant it right here on the earth where most of us can get a slice of it. It isn't as pretty a heaven —there aren't any streets of gold and there aren't any angels, and we'd have to worry about sewerage, and railroad schedules in it, and we don't guarantee everybody'd love it, but it'd be right here, stuck in the mud of this earth, and there wouldn't be any entrance requirement, like dying, to get into it.... Dead or alive, I see that, and it won't let me rest. I was the first one to get up in this black grave of ours, because that idea wouldn't let me rest. I pulled the others with me—that's my job, pulling the others ... They only know what they want—I know how they can get it....

KATHERINE

There's still the edge of arrogance on you.

DRISCOLL

I got heaven in my two hands to give to men. There's reason for arrogance....

KATHERINE

I came to ask you to lie down and let them bury you. It seems foolish now. But ...

DRISCOLL

It's foolish, Katherine. I didn't get up from the dead to go back to the dead. I'm going to the living now....

KATHERINE

Fifteen years. It's a good thing your mother isn't alive. How can you say good-bye to a dead brother, Tom?

DRISCOLL

Wish him an easy grave, Katherine....

KATHERINE

A green and pleasant grave to you, Tom, when, finally . . . finally . . . green and pleasant. (*Blackout.*)

The spotlight illuminates PRIVATE DEAN, *the* SIXTH CORPSE, *where he stands with his back to the audience, listening to his mother, a thin, shabby, red-eyed woman of about forty-five, sitting above and to the right, in the full glare of the spotlight.* DEAN *is in shadow.*

MRS. DEAN

Let me see your face, son . . .

DEAN

You don't want to see it, mom . . .

MRS. DEAN

My baby's face. Once, before you . . .

DEAN

You don't want to see it, mom. I know. Didn't they tell you what happened to me?

MRS. DEAN

I asked the doctor. He said a piece of shell hit the side of your head—but even so. . . .

DEAN

Don't ask to see it, mom.

MRS. DEAN

How are you, son? (DEAN *laughs a little—bitterly*) Oh, I forgot. I asked you that question so many times while you were growing up, Jimmy. Let me see your face, Jimmy—just once. . . .

DEAN

How did Alice take it when she heard . . . ?

MRS. DEAN

She put a gold star in her window. She tells everybody you were going to be married. Is that so?

DEAN

Maybe. I liked Alice.

MRS. DEAN

She came over on your birthday. That was before this—this happened. She brought flowers. Big chrysanthemums. Yellow. A lot of them. We had to put them in two vases. I baked a cake. I don't know why. It's hard to get eggs and fine flour nowadays. My baby, twenty years old . . . Let me see your face, Jimmy, boy. . . .

DEAN

Go home, mom. . . . It's not doing you any good staying here. . . .

MRS. DEAN

I want you to let them bury you, Baby. It's done now and over. It would be better for you that way. . . .

DEAN

There's no better to it, mom—and no worse. It happened that way, that's all.

MRS. DEAN

Let me see your face, Jimmy. You had such a fine face. Like a good baby's. It hurt me when you started to shave. Somehow, I almost forget what you looked like, Baby. I remember what you looked like when you were five, when you were ten—you were chubby and fair and your cheeks felt like little silk cushions when I put my hand on them. But I don't remember how you looked when you went away with that uniform on you and that helmet over your face. . . . Baby, let me see your face, once. . . .

DEAN

Don't ask me . . . You don't want to see. You'll feel worse—forever . . . if you see . . .

MRS. DEAN

I'm not afraid. I can look at my baby's face. Do you think mothers can be frightened by their children's . . .

DEAN

No, mom . . .

MRS. DEAN

Baby, listen to me, I'm your mother. . . . Let them bury you. There's something peaceful and done about a grave. After a while you forget the death and you remember only the life before it. But this way—you never forget... it's a wound walking around forever, without peace. For your sake and mine and your father's ... Baby ...

DEAN

I was only twenty, mom. I hadn't done anything. I hadn't seen anything. I never even had a girl. I spent twenty years practising to be a man and then they killed me. Being a kid's no good, mom. You try to get over it as soon as you can. You don't really live while you're a kid. You mark time, waiting. I waited, mom—but then I got cheated. They made a speech and played a trumpet and dressed me in a uniform and then they killed me.

MRS. DEAN

Oh, Baby, Baby, there's no peace this way. Please, let them ...

DEAN

No, mom ...

MRS. DEAN

Then once, now, so that I can remember—let me see your face, my baby's face ...

DEAN

Mom, the shell hit close to me. You don't want to look at a man when a shell hits close to him.

MRS. DEAN

Let me see your face, Jimmy...

DEAN

All right, mom...Look! (*He turns his face to her. The audience can't see his face, but immediately a spotlight, white and sharp, shoots down from directly above and hits* DEAN's *head.* MRS. DEAN *leans forward, staring. Another spotlight shoots down immediately after from the extreme right, then one from the left, then two more, from above. They hit with the impact of blows and* MRS. DEAN *shudders a little as they come, as though she were watching her son being beaten. There is absolute silence for a moment. Then* MRS. DEAN *starts to moan, low, painfully. The lights remain fixed and* MRS. DEAN's *moans rise to a wail, then to a scream. She leans back, covering her eyes with her hands, screaming. Blackout. The scream persists, fading, like a siren fading in the distance, until it is finally stilled.*)

> *The spotlight on* CORPSE THREE, PRIVATE WEBSTER, *and his wife, a dumpy, sad little woman.*

MARTHA WEBSTER

Say something.

WEBSTER

What do you want me to say?

MARTHA

Something—anything. Only talk. You give me the shivers standing there like that—looking like that. . . .

WEBSTER

Even now—after this—there's nothing that we can talk to each other about.

MARTHA

Don't talk like that. You talked like that enough when you were alive— It's not my fault that you're dead. . . .

WEBSTER

No.

MARTHA

It was bad enough when you were alive—and you didn't talk to me and you looked at me as though I was always in your way.

WEBSTER

Martha, Martha, what's the difference now?

MARTHA

I just wanted to let you know. Now I suppose you're going to come back and sit around and ruin my life altogether?

WEBSTER

No. I'm not going to come back.

MARTHA

Then what . . . ?

WEBSTER

I couldn't explain it to you, Martha. . . .

MARTHA

No! Oh, no—you couldn't explain it to your
wife. But you could explain it to that dirty
bunch of loafers down at that damned garage of
yours and you could explain it to those bums in
the saloon on F Street. . . .

WEBSTER

I guess I could. (*Musing*) Things seemed to be
clearer when I was talking to the boys while I
worked over a job. And I managed to talk
so people could get to understand what I meant
down at the saloon on F Street. It was nice,
standing there of a Saturday night, with a beer
in front of you and a man or two that under-
stood your own language next to you, talking—
oh, about Babe Ruth or the new oiling system
Ford was putting out or the chances of us gettin'
into the war. . . .

MARTHA

It's different if you were rich and had a fine
beautiful life you wanted to go back to. Then I
could understand. But you were poor . . . you always had dirt under your finger nails, you never
ate enough, you hated me, your wife, you

couldn't stand being in the same room with me.
... Don't shake your head, I know. Out of your
whole life, all you could remember that's good
is a beer on Saturday night that you drank in
company with a couple of bums. ...

WEBSTER

That's enough. I didn't think about it then ...
but I guess I was happy those times.

MARTHA

You were happy those times ... but you weren't
happy in your own home! I know, even if you
don't say it! Well, I wasn't happy either! Living in three damned rooms that the sun didn't
hit five times a year! Watching the roaches
make picnics on the walls! Happy!

WEBSTER

I did my best.

MARTHA

Eighteen-fifty a week! Your best! Eighteen-
fifty, condensed milk, a two-dollar pair of shoes
once a year, five hundred dollars' insurance,
chopped meat. God, how I hate chopped meat!
Eighteen-fifty, being afraid of everything—
of the landlord, the gas company, scared stiff
every month that I was goin' to have a baby!
Why shouldn't I have a baby? Who says I
shouldn't have a baby? Eighteen-fifty, no baby!

WEBSTER

I woulda liked a kid.

MARTHA

Would you? You never said anything.

WEBSTER

It's good to have a kid. A kid's somebody to talk
to.

MARTHA

At first...In the beginning...I thought we'd
have a kid some day.

WEBSTER

Yeah, me too. I used to go out on Sundays and
watch men wheel their kids through the park.

MARTHA

There were so many things you didn't tell me.
Why did you keep quiet?

WEBSTER

I was ashamed to talk to you. I couldn't give you
anything.

MARTHA

I'm sorry.

WEBSTER

In the beginning it looked so fine. I used to smile
to myself when I walked beside you in the street
and other men looked at you.

MARTHA

That was a long time ago.

WEBSTER

A kid would've helped.

MARTHA

No, it wouldn't. Don't fool yourself, Webster. The Clarks downstairs have four and it doesn't help them. Old man Clark comes home drunk every Saturday night and beats 'em with his shaving strap and throws plates at the old lady. Kids don't help the poor. Nothing helps the poor! I'm too smart to have sick, dirty kids on eighteen-fifty....

WEBSTER

That's it....

MARTHA

A house should have a baby. But it should be a clean house with a full icebox. Why shouldn't I have a baby? Other people have babies. Even now, with the war, other people have babies. They don't have to feel their skin curl every time they tear a page off the calendar. They go off to beautiful hospitals in lovely ambulances and have babies between colored sheets! What's there about them that God likes that He makes it so easy for *them* to have babies?

WEBSTER

They're not married to mechanics.

MARTHA

No! It's not eighteen-fifty for them. And now

... now it's worse. Your twenty dollars a month. You hire yourself out to be killed and I get twenty dollars a month. I wait on line all day to get a loaf of bread. I've forgotten what butter tastes like. I wait on line with the rain soaking through my shoes for a pound of rotten meat once a week. At night I go home. Nobody to talk to, just sitting, watching the bugs, with one little light because the Government's got to save electricity. You had to go off and leave me to that! What's the war to me that I have to sit at night with nobody to talk to? What's the war to you that you had to go off and ... ?

WEBSTER

That's why I'm standing up now, Martha.

MARTHA

What took you so long, then? Why now? Why not a month ago, a year ago, ten years ago? Why didn't you stand up then? Why wait until you're dead? You live on eighteen-fifty a week, with the roaches, not saying a word, and then when they kill you, you stand up! You fool!

WEBSTER

I didn't see it before.

MARTHA

Just like you! Wait until it's too late! There's plenty for live men to stand up for!

All right, stand up! It's about time you talked back. It's about time all you poor miserable eighteen-fifty bastards stood up for themselves and their wives and the children they can't have! Tell 'em *all* to stand up! Tell 'em! *Tell 'em!* (*She shrieks. Blackout.*)

A spotlight picks out the FIRST GENERAL. *He has his hands to his lips.*

FIRST GENERAL

It didn't work. But keep it quiet. For God's sake, keep it quiet. . . . (*Blackout.*)

A spotlight picks out the newspaper office, the REPORTER *and the* EDITOR.

REPORTER
(*In harsh triumph*)

It didn't work! Now, you've got to put it in! I knew it wouldn't work! Smear it over the head-lines! It didn't work!

EDITOR

Put it in the headlines. . . . They won't be buried! (*Blackout—Voices call. . . .*)

VOICE
(NEWSBOY *spotted*)

It didn't work! Extra! It didn't work!

VOICE

(*In dark. Hoarse whisper*)

It didn't work! They're still standing.... Somebody do something....

VOICE

(*Spotted, a clubwoman type*)

Somebody do something....

VOICE

(NEWSBOY *spotted*)

Extra! They're still standing....

VOICE

(CLUBWOMAN)

Don't let them back into the country....

REPORTER

(*Spotted. Triumphantly*)

They're standing. From now on they'll always stand! You can't bury soldiers any more.... (*Spotted, a group, owners of the next four voices.*)

VOICE

They stink. Bury them!

VOICE

What are we going to do about them?

VOICE

What'll happen to our war? We can't let anything happen to our war....

VOICE
(*A* PRIEST, *facing the three men*)
Pray! Pray! God must help us! Down on your
knees, all of you and pray with your hearts and
your guts and the marrow of your bones. . . .

VOICE
(REPORTER *spotted, facing them all*)
It will take more than prayers. What are pray-
ers to a dead man? They're standing! Mankind
is standing up and climbing out of its grave.
. . . (*Blackout.*)

VOICE
(*In dark*)
Have you heard. . . ? It didn't work. . . .

VOICE
(*In dark*)
Extra! Extra! It didn't work! They're still
standing! (*Spotted,* MRS. DEAN, MRS. SCHEL-
LING, JULIA BLAKE.)

MRS. DEAN
My baby. . . .

MRS. SCHELLING
My husband. . . .

JULIA BLAKE
My lover. . . .
(*Blackout.*)

VOICE
(*In dark*)

Bury them! They stink!
(*The next set of characters walks through a stationary spotlight.*)

VOICE
(*A* FARMER)

Plant a new crop! The old crop has worn out the earth. Plant something besides lives in the old and weary earth....

VOICE
(*A* NEWSBOY, *running*)

Extra! It didn't work!

VOICE
(*A* BANKER. *Frantic*)

Somebody do something! Dupont's passed a dividend!

VOICE
(*A* PRIEST)

The Day of Judgment is at hand....

VOICE
(*The* FIRST WHORE)

Where is Christ?
(*Blackout.*)

VOICE
(*In dark*)

File 'em away in alphabetical order....
(*Spotlight on a man in academic robes, reading*

aloud from behind a table, after he adjusts his glasses.)

VOICE

We don't believe it. It is against the dictates of science. (*Blackout—Spot on* SECOND GENERAL.)

SECOND GENERAL

Keep it quiet!
(MRS. SCHELLING *walks in front of him. The others follow.*)

BESS SCHELLING

My husband....

JULIA BLAKE

My lover....

MRS. DEAN

My baby.... (*Blackout.*)

VOICE
(*A* CHILD)

What have they done with my father?
(*Spot on* BANKER *at telephone.*)

BANKER
(*Into phone*)

Somebody do something. Call up the War Department! Call up Congress! Call up the Roman Catholic Church! Somebody do something!

VOICE

We've got to put them down!

REPORTER
(*Spotted*)

Never! Never! Never! You can't put them down. Put one down and ten will spring up like weeds in an old garden.... (*Spots at various parts of the stage.*)

VOICE
(*The* THIRD GENERAL)

Use lead on them, lead! Lead put 'em down once, lead'll do it again! Lead!

VOICE

Put down the sword and hang the armor on the wall to rust with the years. The killed have arisen.

VOICE

Bury them! Bury the dead!

VOICE

The old demons have come back to possess the earth. We are lost....

VOICE

The dead have arisen, now let the living rise, singing....

VOICE

Do something, for the love of God, do something....

VOICE

Extra! They're still standing.

VOICE

Do something!

VOICE
(*In dark*)
We will do something. . . .

VOICE

Who are you?

VOICE
(PRIEST *in spot*)
We are the Church and the voice of God. The State has tried its ways, now let the Church use the ways of God. These corpses are possessed by the devil, who plagues the lives of men. The Church will exorcise the devil from these men, according to its ancient rite, and they will lie down in their graves like children to a pleasant sleep, rising no more to trouble the world of living men. The Church which is the Voice of God upon this earth, amen. . . . (*Blackout.*)

CHORUS OF VOICES

Alleluia, alleluia, sing. . . . (*The scream of the bereft mother fades in, reaches its height, then dies off as the holy procession of priests moves solemnly on with bell, book and candle. A* PRIEST *sprinkles the* CORPSES *with holy water, makes the sign of the cross over them and begins in the solemn Latin of the service. At the end he goes into English—his voice rising in ritualistic passion.*)

PRIEST

I exorcise thee, unclean spirit, in the name of Jesus Christ; tremble, O Satan, thou enemy of the faith, thou foe of mankind, who hast brought death into the world, who hast deprived men of life, and hast rebelled against justice, thou seducer of mankind, thou root of evil, thou source of avarice, discord, and envy. (*Silence. Then the* CORPSES *begin to laugh, lightly, horribly. There is a sign from the living men present, and the priestly procession goes off, its bell tinkling. The laughter goes on. Blackout. The* VOICES *call again....*)

VOICE

No....

VOICE

NO!

VOICE

It didn't work....

VOICE

We are deserted by God for our evil ways. It is the new flood, without rain....

NEWSBOY

They're licked.

VOICE

This isn't 1918! This is today!

VOICE

See what happens tomorrow!

VOICE

Anything can happen now! Anything!

VOICE

They're coming. We must stop them!

VOICE

We must find ways, find means!

VOICE
(*The* REPORTER, *exulting*)

They're coming! There will be no ways, no means!

SEMI-CHORUS
(*Mocking*)

What are you going to do?

CHORUS

What are you going to do? (*They laugh sardonically.*)

THIRD GENERAL

Let me have a machine gun! Sergeant! A machine gun! (*A bolt of light comes down to a machine gun set to the left of the grave, mid-way between the edge of the grave and the wings. The* GENERALS *are clustered around it.*)

THIRD GENERAL

I'll show them! This is what they've needed!

FIRST GENERAL

All right, all right. Get it over with! Hurry! But keep it quiet!

THIRD GENERAL

I want a crew to man this gun. (*Pointing to* FIRST SOLDIER) You! Come over here! And you! You know what to do. I'll give the command to fire. . . .

FIRST SOLDIER

Not to me, you won't. . . . This is over me. I won't touch that gun. None of us will! We didn't hire out to be no butcher of dead men. Do your own chopping. . . .

THIRD GENERAL

You'll be court-martialed! You'll be dead by tomorrow morning. . . .

FIRST SOLDIER

Be careful, General! I may take a notion to come up like these guys. That's the smartest thing I've seen in this army. I like it. . . . (*To* DRISCOLL) What d'ye say, Buddy?

DRISCOLL

It's about time. . . . (*The* THIRD GENERAL *draws his gun, but the other* GENERALS *hold his arm.*)

FIRST GENERAL

Stop it! It's bad enough as it is! Let him alone! do it yourself! Go ahead, do it!

THIRD GENERAL

(*Whispers*)

Oh, my God.... (*He looks down at gun, then slowly gets down on one knee behind it. The other* GENERALS *slide out behind him. The* CORPSES *come together in the middle of the grave, all facing the gun.* THIRD GENERAL *fumbles with the gun.* VOICES *call.*)

REPORTER

Never, never, never!

JULIA

Walter Morgan, Beloved of Julia Blake, Born 1913, Died 1937.

MRS. DEAN

Let me see your face, Baby?

MARTHA WEBSTER

All you remember is a glass of beer with a couple of bums on Saturday night.

KATHERINE DRISCOLL

A green and pleasant grave...

BESS SCHELLING

Did it hurt much, John? His hair is blond and he weighs twenty-eight pounds.

JOAN

You loved me best, didn't you, Henry?... best...

VOICE

Four yards of bloody mud...

VOICE

I understand how they feel, Charlie. I wouldn't
like to be underground ... now ...

REPORTER

Never, never!

VOICE

Never!

MARTHA WEBSTER

Tell 'em all to stand up! Tell 'em! *Tell 'em!*

(*The* CORPSES *begin to walk toward the left
end of the grave, not marching, but walking together, silently. The* THIRD GENERAL
*stiffens, then starts to laugh hysterically. As
the* CORPSES *reach the edge of the grave and
take their first step out, he starts firing, laughing
wildly, the gun shaking his shoulders violently.
Calmly, in the face of the chattering gun, the*
CORPSES *gather on the brink of the grave, then
walk soberly, in a little bunch, toward the* THIRD
GENERAL. *For a moment they obscure him as
they pass him. In that moment the gun stops.
There is absolute silence. The* CORPSES *pass on,
going off the stage, like men who have leisurely
business that must be attended to in the not too
pressing future. As they pass the gun, they re-*

veal the THIRD GENERAL, *slumped forward, still, over the still gun. There is no movement on the stage for a fraction of a second. Then, slowly, the* FOUR SOLDIERS *of the burial detail break ranks. Slowly they walk, exactly as the* CORPSES *have walked, off toward the left, past the* THIRD GENERAL. *The last* SOLDIER, *as he passes the* THIRD GENERAL, *deliberately, but without malice, flicks a cigarette butt at him, then follows the other* SOLDIERS *off the stage. The* THIRD GENERAL *is the last thing we see, huddled over his quiet gun, pointed at the empty grave, as the light dims—in the silence.*)

Curtain